W9-DJQ-326

SUPER SIMPLE

THANKSGIVING

ACTIVITIES

FUN AND EASY HOLIDAY PROJECTS FOR KIDS

Megan Borgert-Spaniol

Consulting Editor, Diane Craig, M.A./Reading Specialist

Super Sandcastle

An Imprint of Abdo Publishing
abdopublishing.com

abdopublishing.com

Published by Abdo Publishing, a division of ABDO, PO Box 398166, Minneapolis, Minnesota 55439.
Copyright © 2018 by Abdo Consulting Group, Inc. International copyrights reserved in all countries.
No part of this book may be reproduced in any form without written permission from the publisher.
Super SandCastle™ is a trademark and logo of Abdo Publishing.

Printed in the United States of America, North Mankato, Minnesota

102017
012018

 THIS BOOK CONTAINS
RECYCLED MATERIALS

Design: Alison Stuerman, Mighty Media, Inc.
Production: Mighty Media, Inc.
Editor: Rebecca Felix
Cover Photographs: Mighty Media, Inc.; Shutterstock
Interior Photographs: Mighty Media, Inc.; Shutterstock

The following manufacturers/names appearing in this book are trademarks: Bostitch®, Craft Smart®,
Mod Podge®, Rolo®, Scotch®, Sharpie®

Publisher's Cataloging-in-Publication Data
Names: Borgert-Spaniol, Megan, author.
Title: Super simple Thanksgiving activities: fun and easy holiday projects for kids /
by Megan Borgert-Spaniol.
Other titles: Fun and easy holiday projects for kids
Description: Minneapolis, Minnesota : Abdo Publishing, 2018. | Series: Super simple holidays |
Identifiers: LCCN 2017946527 | ISBN 9781532112478 (lib.bdg.) | ISBN 9781614799894 (ebook)
Subjects: LCSH: Thanksgiving decorations--Juvenile literature. | Handicraft--Juvenile literature. |
    Holiday decorations--Juvenile literature.
Classification: DDC 745.5941649--dc23
LC record available at https://lccn.loc.gov/2017946527

Super SandCastle™ books are created by a team of professional educators, reading specialists,
and content developers around five essential components—phonemic awareness, phonics,
vocabulary, text comprehension, and fluency—to assist young readers as they develop reading
skills and strategies and increase their general knowledge. All books are written, reviewed,
and leveled for guided reading and early reading intervention for use in shared, guided, and
independent reading and writing activities to support a balanced approach to literacy instruction.

TO ADULT HELPERS

The craft projects in this series are
fun and simple. There are just a
few things to remember to keep
kids safe. Some projects require
the use of hot objects or food
items with allergy triggers. Also,
kids may be using messy materials
such as glue or paint. Make sure
they protect their clothes and
work surfaces. Review the projects
before starting and be ready to
assist when necessary.

KEY SYMBOLS

Watch for these warning symbols in this
book. Here is what each one means.

 HOT!
This project requires the use
of a stove or oven. Get help!

 NUTS!
This project includes the use
of nuts. Find out whether
anyone you are serving has
a nut allergy.

CONTENTS 🍁

HAPPY HOLIDAYS!

Holidays are great times to celebrate with family and friends. Many people have favorite holiday **traditions**. Some traditions are hundreds of years old. But people start new traditions too, such as making holiday foods and crafts.

THANKSGIVING

Thanksgiving is a day of **gratitude**. Europeans arrived in New England in 1620. Native Americans taught them to grow corn. In 1621, both groups shared a meal to celebrate the harvest.

This was the first American Thanksgiving. Today, Americans celebrate this holiday on the fourth Thursday of November. They gather to give thanks for food, peace, and community.

CELEBRATE THANKSGIVING

Many Thanksgiving **traditions** are common in homes across the country. How do you celebrate Thanksgiving?

FEAST

The first Thanksgiving featured corn, **fowl**, **shellfish**, and deer meat. Today, turkey is the main food at this holiday. People also often eat potatoes, cranberries, and pumpkin pie.

GIVING BACK

For many, Thanksgiving is a time to help their communities. People serve meals to the homeless. They also **donate** food to those in need.

FAMILY TIME

Many people travel hundreds of miles to be with loved ones for Thanksgiving. It is common for families to watch football together on this day. They also play games and enjoy parades.

MATERIALS

Here are some of the materials that you will need for the projects in this book.

BAKING SHEET	CANDY CORN	CARD STOCK	CARDBOARD	CHENILLE STEMS	CLEAR TAPE
COLORED PAPER	CRAFT GLUE	FELT	GOOGLY EYES	HOLE PUNCH	MARKERS

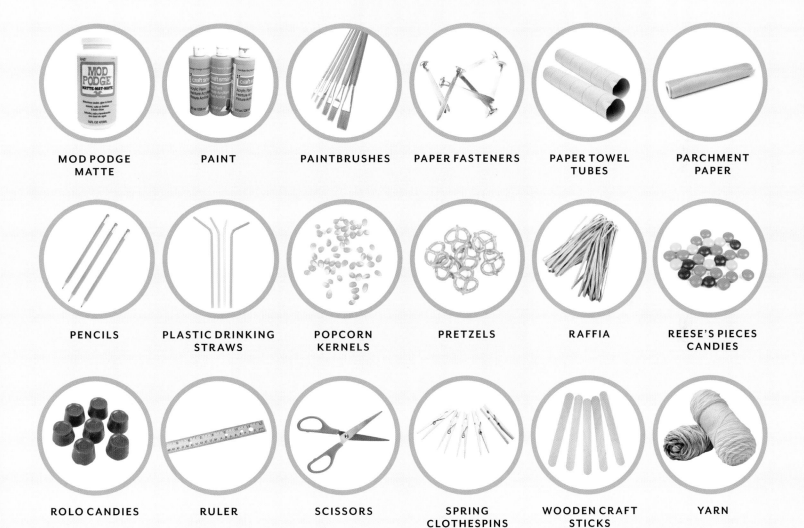

MOD PODGE
MATTE

PAINT

PAINTBRUSHES

PAPER FASTENERS

PAPER TOWEL
TUBES

PARCHMENT
PAPER

PENCILS

PLASTIC DRINKING
STRAWS

POPCORN
KERNELS

PRETZELS

RAFFIA

REESE'S PIECES
CANDIES

ROLO CANDIES

RULER

SCISSORS

SPRING
CLOTHESPINS

WOODEN CRAFT
STICKS

YARN

THUMBPRINT TURKEY CARD
Create a handcrafted Thanksgiving greeting!

WHAT YOU NEED

card stock

scissors

newspaper

yellow, orange, red &
    brown paint

paper towels

craft glue

googly eyes

small paintbrush

markers

1 Fold a sheet of card stock in half crosswise. Cut along the fold. Then fold one piece in half crosswise to make a card.

2 Cover your work surface with newspaper. Put a small dab of each paint color on it.

3 Dip your thumb in yellow paint. Stamp your thumb on the card several times to form an arc.

4 Clean your thumb. Dip it in orange paint. Stamp an orange arc below the yellow arc.

5 Clean your thumb. Dip it in red paint. Stamp a red arc below the orange arc.

6 Clean your thumb. Dip it in brown paint. Stamp once below the red arc. Stamp the tip of your thumb above the brown stamp.

7 Glue googly eyes onto the turkey. Paint its beak and legs. Once the paint dries, write in your card and send it someone!

THANKSGIVING GARLAND

Weave autumn leaves into festive trimmings!

12

1 Cut the plastic straws into ¾-inch (2 cm) pieces. You will need one straw piece for each leaf.

2 Tape a straw piece to the back of each leaf.

3 Tape a toothpick to the end of the yarn.

4 Thread the yarn through each straw piece.

5 Hang your **garland** to celebrate the Thanksgiving season!

TURKEY TREATS

Bake sweet turkey treats that are fun to gobble up!

WHAT YOU NEED
baking sheet
parchment paper
pretzels
ROLO candies
oven mitts
white jumbo
  sprinkles
toothpick
Reese's Pieces
  candies
candy corn

1 Heat the oven to 300 **degrees** Fahrenheit.

2 Line the baking sheet with parchment paper. Arrange the pretzels on the sheet.

3 Place a ROLO on each pretzel near the edge with two curves. Bake the sheet for 1 to 2 minutes.

4 Place two sprinkles on each ROLO as shown. Be careful not to touch the hot baking sheet! Dip a toothpick into each ROLO. Dot melted chocolate onto each sprinkle. These are the turkeys' eyes.

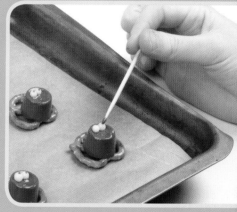

5 Place one Reese's Pieces candy below each set of eyes. These are the turkeys' beaks.

6 Push three pieces of candy corn into the side of each ROLO to make feathers. Be careful not to touch the hot baking sheet!

7 Let the chocolate cool, then enjoy!

GOOFY GOBBLER
CHARADES
This turkey's feathers hold all you need
for a fun Thanksgiving game!

WHAT YOU NEED

newspaper

10–15 wooden craft
  sticks

yellow, red &
  orange paint

paintbrush

small drinking glass

marker

brown paper

scissors

clear tape

red & orange felt

craft glue

googly eyes

popcorn kernels

1 Cover your work surface with newspaper. Paint one side of 10 to 15 craft sticks yellow. Let the paint dry.

2 Cut a strip of brown paper as wide as the glass is tall. Roll the paper into a **cylinder**. Make sure it covers the inside of the glass. Tape the cylinder together.

3 Draw a turkey neck and head shape on another piece of brown paper. Cut the shape out.

4 Cut a beak out of orange felt. Cut a **wattle** out of red felt. Glue these features to the turkey's face. Add googly eyes.

(continued on next page)

5 Tape the turkey head to the paper **cylinder**. Fit the turkey into the glass.

6 Fill the glass three-fourths full with popcorn kernels.

7 Write Thanksgiving-related words or phrases on the yellow sides of the craft sticks.

Pumpkin Pie

Football

8 Decorate the other sides of the craft sticks. Paint them yellow, red, and orange. Let the paint dry.

9 Draw lines on the craft stick sides you just painted to make them look like turkey feathers.

10 Push the craft sticks into the popcorn kernels. Place them so the words are not visible when looking at the turkey.

11 Play charades with friends and family! Take turns pulling a stick from the glass. Silently act out the word or phrase written on the stick. The other players must guess the word or phrase.

TIP Don't have popcorn kernels? Fill the glass with dry rice or beans instead.

9

10

GRATITUDE WREATH

Give thanks with a colorful clothespin wreath!

WHAT YOU NEED

newspaper

red, orange & yellow paint

paintbrush

50–55 spring clothespins of various sizes

10-inch (25 cm) craft ring

marker

colored paper

scissors

ruler

string

clear tape

20

1 Cover your work surface with newspaper. Paint the clothespins red, orange, and yellow. Let the paint dry.

2 Clip the clothespins to the craft ring.

3 Write "Thankful" on colored paper. Cut around the word to make a sign.

4 Cut a 12-inch (31 cm) piece of string. Tape the sign to the center of the string.

5 Lay the string across the wreath. Secure each end of the string to the ring with a clothespin.

6 Draw several leaf shapes on colored paper. Cut them out. Write something you are thankful for on each leaf.

7 Use the clothespins to secure the leaves to the wreath. Then hang your work of art for all to see!

21

AUTUMN GLOW JAR

Watch warm candlelight give autumn leaves a cozy glow!

WHAT YOU NEED

smooth-sided jar

Mod Podge Matte

foam brush

fall leaves (real or artificial)

raffia

scissors

small battery-powered candle

1 Coat the outside of the jar with Mod Podge Matte.

2 Stick a leaf to the jar. Brush Mod Podge Matte over the leaf.

3 Place another leaf on the jar. It should slightly **overlap** the first leaf. Brush Mod Podge Matte over the leaf.

4 Repeat step 3 until the jar is covered with leaves. Let the Mod Podge dry.

5 Cut a long piece of raffia. Wrap it several times around the top of the jar. Tie the ends together.

6 Turn on a small battery-powered candle and place it in the jar. Watch your autumn leaves begin to glow!

COLORFUL
CORN BOUQUET

Create a corn bouquet that represents the autumn harvest!

WHAT YOU NEED

ruler

marker

cardboard

scissors

raffia

stapler

newspaper

red, yellow,
  orange &
  brown paint

card stock

pencils with
  erasers

craft glue

24

1 Use a marker and ruler to draw a *T* shape on the cardboard. Cut the shape out.

2 Measure 12 inches (31 cm) of raffia. Do not cut it. Fold the length of raffia in half to form a **loop**. Hold the ends together.

3 Repeat step 2, measuring and folding until you have a thick **bouquet** of raffia loops. Cut the raffia from the roll.

4 Pull the last piece of raffia loose from the bouquet. Hold the bouquet together at one end. Wrap the loose piece of raffia around this end several times. Then tie it in a knot around the bouquet.

(continued on next page)

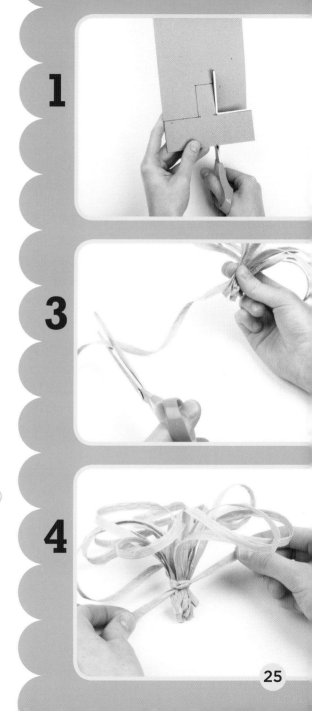

5 Cut the raffia **loops** open at the top.

6 Place the cardboard so the *T* shape is upside down. Staple the raffia **bouquet** to the vertical part of the *T*.

7 Cut a piece of raffia 12 inches (31 cm) long. Staple one end below the bottom of the raffia bouquet.

8 Wrap the raffia piece from step 7 around the bouquet to hide the staples. Staple the other end of the piece to the cardboard to secure it.

9 Cover your work surface in newspaper. Place a small dab of each color of paint on the newspaper.

10 Dip a pencil eraser in red paint. Stamp red dots onto a sheet of card stock.

11 Repeat step 10 with the yellow, orange, and brown paint. Let the paint dry.

12 Draw a **corncob** shape on cardboard. Cut out the shape. This is a **template**.

13 Trace the template three times on the painted card stock. Cut out the shapes.

14 Glue one corncob to the **horizontal** part of the *T*, near the center. Add one corncob on either side. The corncobs should **overlap**.

15 Display your corn decoration during the Thanksgiving season!

TIP Autumn corn comes in many colors. Mix paint colors to make new shades!

YARN
NAPKIN RINGS

Make Thanksgiving dinner guests their own reusable napkin rings!

WHAT YOU NEED

ruler

paper towel tube

scissors

yarn in various colors

tape

colored paper

marker

craft glue

28

1 Cut the paper towel tube into 2-inch (5 cm) sections.

2 Cut a long piece of yarn.

3 Tie one end of the yarn around the side of a tube piece. Tape the knot to the inside of the tube.

4 Wrap the yarn around the sides of the paper tube. Make sure the yarn rows completely cover the tube.

5 Repeat steps 3 and 4 whenever you run out of yarn or want to change colors. Tie or tuck in any loose ends.

6 Cut a small rectangle out of colored paper. Write someone's name on it. Glue the name tag to the napkin ring.

7 Repeat steps 2 through 6 to make several personalized napkin rings. Then use them to set your Thanksgiving table!

29

PLUMP
PAPER PUMPKIN

This roly-poly gourd makes a great
centerpiece for your Thanksgiving table!

WHAT YOU NEED

orange paper

ruler

scissors

hole punch

paper fasteners

brown & green
   chenille stems

1 Cut the orange paper **lengthwise** into 15 strips. Make each strip 1 inch (2.5 cm) wide.

2 Punch a hole at both ends of each strip.

3 **Stack** the strips so their holes match up.

4 Stick a paper fastener through each set of holes. Flatten each fastener.

5 Fan out the orange strips into a globe.

6 Make a pumpkin stem and vine with the chenille stems. Wrap their ends around the top paper fastener.

7 Display your pumpkin during your Thanksgiving feast!

2

4

5

GLOSSARY

bouquet – a bunch of flowers or plants gathered together or arranged in a vase.

corncob – an ear of corn.

cylinder – a solid, round shape with flat ends. A soda can is a cylinder.

degree – the unit used to measure temperature.

donate – to give a gift in order to help others.

fowl – a bird, such as a duck, goose, turkey, or chicken, that is eaten or hunted.

garland – a decorative ring or rope made of leaves, flowers, or some other material.

gratitude – a feeling of being thankful or grateful.

horizontal – in the same direction as, or parallel to, the ground.

lengthwise – in the direction of the longest side.

loop – a circle made by a rope, string, or thread.

overlap – to lie partly on top of something.

shellfish – an aquatic animal that has a hard shell, such as a clam or lobster.

stack – to put things on top of each other.

template – a shape or pattern that is drawn or cut around to make the same shape in another material.

tradition – a belief or practice passed through a family or group of people.

wattle – the flap of skin that hangs from the neck of some birds.